HYPERACTIVE CHILDREN
– a parents guide

HYPERACTIVE CHILDREN
– a parents guide

Shirley Flack

BISHOPSGATE PRESS

Cover photograph by Steve Shipman

© 1987 Shirley Flack

British Library Cataloguing in Publication Data

Flack, Shirley
   Hyperactive children : a parents guide.
   1. Hyperactive children
   I. Title
   618.92'8589   RJ506.H9

ISBN 1 85219 005 1

All rights reserved. No part of this publication may be reproduced, stored in a retrieval system, or transmitted, in any form or by any means, electronic, mechanical, photocopying, recording or otherwise, without the prior permission of the Publishers.

All enquiries and requests relevant to this title should be sent to the publisher, Bishopsgate Press Ltd., 37 Union Street, London SE1 1SE

Printed by Whitstable Litho Ltd., Whitstable, Kent.

CONTENTS

Foreword	7
Preface	9
We are what we eat	12
David – 'As driven by a motor'	15
Jennifer – 'The doctors said she was epileptic'	19
Timothy – 'Three or four days on my Evening Primrose oil and my horrible monster son turned into the dearest little boy'	25
Michael – 'Within minutes his eyes started to go very red and sore'	30
The Coopers – 'Just an ordinary family – not hyperactivity, but reacting badly	35
Stephen's mother: 'A lone parent – an impossible burden'	40
Letters to Sally Bunday	47
The problems of metal pollution	59
Is there hyperactivity in adults?	62
The good foods and the bad	68
The sweet bag	78
Useful addresses	86
Further reading	88

DEDICATION

As they get better, children who have been hyperactive very often describe the bad feelings they used to have. Feeling hot and angry, feeling as if your head is buzzing, feeling silly, feeling different from your friends, but most of all feeling unhappy, as if nobody wants you, everybody hates you.

One child identified the horrid, hateful creature who invaded her body as Nellie Beast. Nellie Beast lived in Sugarland so if you kept away from Sugarland Nellie Beast couldn't get you.

This book is dedicated to all the Nellie Beasts who have helped to show us the way out of Sugarland.

To their parents who having persevered to make their children better have chronicled the setbacks and celebrated their successes with advice to others just setting out on the journey.

For other parents who may recognise their own Nellie Beasts in these pages and see their own way out of Sugarland at last.

And also for those of us who have been fortunate because our own children are not among those who may be susceptible to hyperactivity. To help us understand – and, understanding, show sympathy, tolerance and even a little wisdom, when asked.

FOREWORD

A timely book – a message of hope for the guilty, demoralised desperately tired parents who feel like shutting themselves away from society with the "little monster" they produced and reared; whose behaviour, so unlike that which they had anticipated, defies all the orthodox treatments the professionals advised. "Surely, they can't be wrong – it must be our fault" is the parents' common reaction. But they can be and often are because, instead of observing and listening with compassion, they still try to advise and practise only what they were taught.

But there is another way to tackle the problem of these "impossible" children – a way that will not only restore the ebbing loving relationship between parent and child, and the parents' self confidence but a way that is not two difficult for any parent to safely try for themselves.

Before you abandon hope for your "lost" child just take a look at the experiences of others – and if you recognise your child in these pages try to follow the example of their parents as they discovered how to switch off the incorrigible behaviour and moods. I hope those who feel unsympathetic towards these problems will be open-minded enough to learn from the practical "cases" described here. Dare we continue to be so blind? It is sad to think of so many unhappy families whose headlong course into misery and rejection could be so easily changed by a simple change of diet. The evidence is there and we cannot go on ignoring it whilst we wait for the properly designed research to tell us how and why the brain responds to these chemical changes induced by foods and additives in the body. We have a safe method of treatment – why not use it?

Particulary helpful is the diet section. Faced with a list of foods the child should not have, many parents feel inclined to panic and say, "whatever can I give him to eat then?" This section will give them some ideas.

I am very happy to commend this book and to testify that I have used advice similar to this and found it to be effective in my own practice now for several years. It may not always be totally effective, so if it doesn't work, there are other forms of treatment which you can discuss with your doctor.

If is does work, you will not only have saved a lot of professional time, you will have the great satisfaction of restoring normal relationships within your family.

Dr. A. J. Franklin, F.R.C.P., D.C.H
Consultant Paediatrician

PREFACE

In 1985 I was asked to write an article for YOU Magazine, the colour supplement of The Mail of Sunday, on the 'new' and growing syndrome of hyperactivity in children.

The research was absorbing – and the response was overwhelming. Letters came flooding in from readers who, in the main, saw in the article an escape from the isolation that they were enduring. There was a steady flow of requests for additional help and information as the magazine (as is the habit) was passed on, reaching a far wider readership than the original purchasers.

When, on the morning of Christmas Eve, a letter arrived, the timing seemed to heighten its poignancy.

Although several weeks have passed since I read your article, I felt that I must write to thank you for saving our lives. I hope that it brought hope to other people as it did to me and I thank you.

I am the mother of three young sons, 12, 9 and 3 years, so life is very hectic, but my eldest, the 12-year-old, was more trouble than the other two put together.

Simon was always aggressive, a bed-wetter, asthmatic and depressive. He is left-handed, fair haired and fair-skinned, as your article stated.

Recognising him from your description as hyperactive, we immediately sat down and read all the labels on the food, just to see how many E numbers were contained. We were horrified.

We immediately stopped buying any foods containing E numbers at all and the result was amazing.

The aggression stopped. Simon had been trying to hit both myself and my husband with anything he could get his hands on. He was always kicking, spitting and thumping his brother. I had been called to school on several occasions because of his aggressive behaviour to other children and his lack of interest in all school activities.

Before his change of diet he was always depressed and often thought that suicide would be a lot easier because no one wanted him. Now he is a very different boy – no aggression, helpful, loving, happy, good at school and keen on all his lessons. He is sleeping better than he has for years. Most of all, since October there have been no asthma attacks and no need for any drugs.

Although Simon is under the hospital for his asthma, I feel they do not really believe that something as simple as changing his diet could be the answer. But I know and only time will tell.

The bed-wetting is clearing up slowly and with a bit of help from the doctor.

We decided as a family that the best way we could help Simon was for all of us to eat the same, so we all eat food without E numbers. This proved to have an ironic result for my husband also suffered from depression and the new diet has helped him too. His depression has cleared up after trying many things for many years.

I hope my letter will be of help to other people for I was really at my wits' end and trying to cope, nobody understood Simon, just saying he was badly brought up – and we knew different.

I hope that this book, which takes the research that I did for the YOU article very much further, may help other parents at their wits' end over bizarre and violent behaviour, over exhaustion and anger and despair.

It is all about children like Simon – and their parents – and those potentially damaging additives and preservatives which are now incorporated in the food we eat and give our children, with sometimes disastrous results. About the other causes of a condition so destructive and depressing, its effects cannot be contained but overspill far beyond the immediate family group.

What is hyperactivity? How do you recognise it? How do you distinguish between the hyper-active and the over-active child? What do you do about it?

Here is what we know about the problem, its causes and effects, and how parents, but mainly mothers (for when the going gets tough the fathers, sadly but very often, get going) have learned to live with the effects and, happily and increasingly, to win the battle.

WE ARE WHAT WE EAT

It is an old saying, true to a great extent for all but absolutely true of hyperactive children, for whom certain foods are certain poison. One spoonful of the lethal foodstuff, half a glass of the "forbidden" drink and a whole process of responses is triggered off, sometimes within minutes, sometimes the time bomb ticks away until the next day. We will examine those foods and other contributing causes later.

Meanwhile what are the symptoms? The hyperactive child is restless and over-active, excitable and impulsive; disturbs other children; has poor concentration span and fails to finish anything he has started; he is demanding, impatient, easily frustrated; cries often, is moody, explosive, unpredictable and quick tempered; many are poor sleepers, persistent bed-wetters, have poor appetite and excessive thirst. Many are prone to wheezing asthma attacks and irritating rashes. As babies they are fitful with temper tantrums, go in for odd behaviour like head banging, may dribble excessively. As toddlers they are accident prone, a danger to themselves and other children; clumsy and disruptive by the time they reach play group or school. Many seem to have one illness after another, are constantly having to see the doctor for persistent coughs and colds. Some have speech defects and reading difficulties, are invariably poor at organised games and, as they progress through school if that is the right word are identified as "trouble". They are likely to be fair skinned with fair or red hair, left handed and male... hence what may seem a somewhat sexist identification in the preceding list of characteristics. Boys outnumber girls three to one.

Only in recent years have we begun to recognise the link between food and the hyperkinetic syndrome (to give it its medical-psychological term) between what hyperactive children eat and how they behave, between the uncontrollable toddler throwing a tantrum in the supermarket and the chemically loaded contents of the convenience foods in his mother's shopping trolley.

Experience suggests – and increasing evidence confirms – that the chemical additives in our diet today create an allergic reaction, especially in children, that manifests itself in abnormal behaviour. That behaviour is called hyperactivity. It is a symptom of a deep disturbance of the natural metabolic balance in a child. Not that normally active children can't throw a tantrum in the supermarket! But we are not referring here to the boundlessly energetic youngster who always wants to be doing things. We are talking about a hyperactive child with a restless, unco-ordinated, undirected energy. He cannot control or use it positively. Nothing gives him satisfaction. He is deeply unhappy.

People talk of hyperactivity as the disease of our time. No doubt it has always existed, but not in the proportions it has reached in recent years.

There has been very little apparent effort on the part of the National Health Service to research the hyperkinetic syndrome, although it is a growing problem. School headteachers have reported a marked increase in the numbers of small school beginners who, because of their hyperactivity, present serious behaviour problems.

In Britain, one woman, Sally Bunday, has waged a lone campaign against the disease for years, providing a shoulder for parents to cry on and responding with sound advice and support. She has no medical or scientific qualifications, but a wealth of experience and common-sense. Her own son, Miles, was hyperactive and it was because she found an answer for Miles that she wanted to pass on the good news to other parents driven to desperation by the appalling behaviour – and misery – of their children. Now she runs the Hyperactive Children's Support Group (HACSG) from her

Sussex home, distributes pamphlets and "Happiness is junk-free food" badges and travels the country counselling. Much of the information and many of the case histories in the following pages come from Sally's files at the HACSG.

Hyperactivity was officially listed as a disease in the hyperkinetic classification of diseases in the 1940s. In 1980, following a question in the House of Commons, the Minister of Health stated that one in a thousand 10 and 11 year olds was hyperactive. And yet family doctors receive no training in this and many of the letters Sally Bunday receives are from mothers who have found no help whatsoever or, worse, a totally negative approach from their own doctors. GPs don't seem, except in a small minority of cases, to be necessarily better informed than the patient, or the patient's next door neighbour!

One enlightened doctor, who at his clinic sees children referred through schools as having serious behavioural problems, first asks the mother to complete a questionnaire which he receives before he has any direct contact with child or parent. In the last 100 referrals the same phrase appeared in every mother's description of her child – 'as if driven by a motor'.

How does it come about that some children get so hyped up, so revved up and out of control? David was one of them . . .

DAVID – "AS IF DRIVEN BY A MOTOR"

"Emma was 5 when our son, David, was born. He had been very active in the womb. After his birth he was quiet for three days – then he didn't stop for three years. I didn't know what it was to have a night's sleep. I spent the time walking around with him on my shoulder. My husband was very supportive and did what he could but, after all, he was the one who had to get up in the morning to go to work.

David screamed incessantly. People said it was colic, said it was typical for a young baby. But I'd had a baby and I knew this was different. Things got worse when he started to walk. He was non-stop violent and aggressive. Every day you'd think: This can't go on. Surely tomorrow he'll be all right. Apart from my mother, I felt that people blamed me, although not to my face. They'd say things like "Perhaps you're a little tired yourself, edgy. You're making him worse" or "little boys are always a handful aren't they?"

He broke everything he could lay his hands on. It was sheer utter destruction and vandalism. Yet he didn't derive any pleasure from what he'd done. Emma had longed for a baby brother and now she dreaded being with him. Before I had him, I'd seen people shopping with, say, a small child screaming or kicking and I'd thought: What a dreadful mother that she cannot handle her child better than that. But I soon came to see it was hopeless to handle David at all.

I couldn't take him out. I couldn't visit friends with other children. Once we were asked to leave a restaurant in Chichester. I don't blame them really – why should people have to put up with a screaming child while they're eating their lunch?

Holidays were out. We tried because we thought – all that beach, he can run about and use up his energy. But he screamed and whinged and annoyed other people.

My doctor could find no physical reason for his problems and referred me to a paediatrician. Whilst I was waiting for the appointment I heard of Sally Bunday, found out about the diet and at once stopped giving David anything with chemical colouring, preservatives and additives.

I'd been giving him bread with margarine and jam ... both were suspect. He used to consume gallons of Ribena ... that too was suspect, although now they have altered the ingredients.

The effect was incredible. And immediate. Twenty four hours later David slept throughout the night for the first time in 2½ years. A few days later he sat on my knee and I cuddled him and he snuggled up to me for the first time ever.

I still kept the paediatrician's appointment and explained that now I felt my problems were over and why. His expression as he listened to my new 'diet' was total cynicism. "Nonsense," was all he said.

Recently I had a pre-school meeting with the local child care officer. I explained that David is, in fact, a hyperactive child but that I had now learned to control the condition. She smiled in a condescending way. "It's very much the fashion today to have a hyperactive child" was all she said."

Like David the hyperactive child is often born that way: he is restless and fidgety, sleeping only three or four hours a night and crying almost incessantly. The mother, however much she strives to console and comfort and pacify, is helpless. As he gets older his restlessness becomes destructive, his unpredictable behaviour makes him a social risk. The family becomes more exhausted, more isolated, more guilty. The process is inevitable.

GPs tend to prescribe sedatives which only too frequently actually make matters worse. When the child starts school, his behavioural problems get really entrenched. The potential implications are only just becoming known, such as the link between this childhood violence and, say, the violent criminal or soccer hooligan. (There is a distinct link between hyperactivity and baby battering). Cause and effect, or effect and cause?

As the condition has become more common so has the evidence of the link between hyperactivity and food – most suspect being increasingly complex chemical additives. Little Johnny, tearing the place apart, having a screaming tantrum, breaking everything in sight, is not just naughty or spoiled or suffering from a surfeit or absence of motherly love; more likely he's just had a chemical-loaded drink.

Sally Bunday's own son, Miles, presented a daily battle which, were it not so utterly miserable in its effect, would actually sound funny. His endless burrowing to escape via the neighbour's garden into the busy road outside, his preoccupation with the fire, his numerous accidents and emergency dashes to the local casualty centre. (One admission as a patient was short-lived. "Come and take him home. He's too awful to treat" came the request from the ward sister).

By luck, and around the time Miles was being prescribed a succession of drugs, a friend back from a visit to America told Sally about the work being done there by Dr. Ben Feingold, a leading allergist.

Within four days of hearing this and implementing the Feingold Diet as far as she could surmise it, Sally had her first night's sleep. Miles was soon able to sit at the table and eat like the rest of the family. His school behaviour improved.

Sally's marriage, inexorably battered by the trauma that the hyperactive baby imposes, broke down. But her child, simply by changing the food he ate, was cured.

When a woman's magazine ran a feature asking "What chemicals are they putting in our food?" Sally proffered her experience of a healthier son after eliminating the junk. And thereby touched a chord. She had suspected that there would be others, but was not prepared for the avalanche of letters from mothers asking for her advice.

For some time this knowledge was passed along the grapevine, mothers advising other mothers. Her own mother, Irene Colquhoun, assisted her in forming the HACSG in 1977.

Too often the medical profession were slow to see the existence of a link between food and behaviour. As Jennifer's mother found...

JENNIFER – "THE DOCTORS SAID SHE WAS AN EPILEPTIC"

"As a baby our daughter Jennifer was nothing short of a nightmare. She rarely slept more than an hour during the day and often no more than three hours a night. Was always sick after being fed and used to sit in her high chair rocking or banging her head. She did not walk until she was 18 months and only began to speak in simple sentences when she was 2¾ – at the time of the birth of our son.

She had uncontrollable rages and used to smash her toys. She went to a play group and the group leader said that sometimes she seemed to be very bright and above average intelligence, whereas at other times she was unable to do even the simplest things.

She started school at the age of 4¾ and if one of the teachers admired anything she had done she would deliberately destroy it. She had a convulsion shortly after starting school and another six months later. She was put on pheno-barbitone all the time but became extremely violent and wild. The doctor advised increasing the dose, but this only made matters worse. We had to take Jennifer to out-patients at the hospital every month and the doctor there put her on a sedative twice daily. This did not improve matters, but as her brainwave pattern was said to be abnormal we continued with this treatment. By then the doctors said she was an epileptic.

When she was five she had a minor heart operation and her behaviour was unbelievable. She took it all in her stride and made no fuss whatsoever, until she was removed from the Intensive Care Unit into the general ward. We realise now that in intensive care she was not eating anything, but as soon as she was put into the ward she started to eat 'normal' food and reverted back to being extremely difficult and having rages.

A friend gave me a newspaper article concerning the Feingold diet and, without much hope, we wrote for details. We really did not believe that something so simple would help, but by this time we were willing to try anything. After three days following the diet Jennifer actually said "Please" when offered a drink and "Thank you" when it was handed to her. This was the first time in her life she had said please and thank you without tears and tantrums and we were over the moon! She opened the door to a friend of ours and said "Hallo, do come in" and our friend was so surprised she just stood there and stared.

Since then Jennifer has improved beyond our wildest dreams. Of course we still have times when she eats sweets at school, or sucks a felt tip pen and so on, but at least we now KNOW the cause of her bad spells and, more important, she now realises what happens and knows there is nothing she can do until the effect wears off.

This deters her somewhat from eating 'rubbishy' foods. Her school tells us that Jennifer now has the reading age of a 13-14 year old and is up to the standard of most children her age, which is 10 years. Before she began the diet she was hardly able to read anything. She seemed to read her letters in the wrong order – would read NO instead of ON.

The doctor had suggested that we saw a psychologist, but as we were about to start the diet we said no. After following the diet for a couple of months she went back to the hospital and when they had given her tests they said that they no longer wanted to see her and she no longer has to take drugs. Her school is very good and has helped her a lot. We also have a marvellous GP who gives us every support and the feeling that if we have any problems he will be there to help. Since following the 'diet' our other children have been extremely fit and, although our son suffered very badly from chest trouble, he has not had a serious attack for over two years. (We have found such things as orange squash and orange lollies aggravate his condition). In fact, both children managed the past year without a day away from school.

I think the most pleasing result is to realise that after all Jennifer is a normal child and to be able to enjoy her company instead of dreading it.

By the way, she came first in the skipping race at her school sports this year and didn't trip over once! Afterwards she said, "Thank goodness I'm best at something at last!"

Certain key words and phrases crop up when you begin to explore the maze of fact and theory surrounding hyperactivity and top of the list is the name Feingold – one Doctor Benjamin F. of San Francisco, whose work during the Seventies showed a ray of hope to the desperate and inspired a whole series of studies worldwide. He did not invent hyperactivity which has been around for centuries and probably accounts for the fidgetiness of Thomas Edison (described as ineducable) and young Winston Churchill, so difficult to manage that nannies were hired for their physical strength and stalwart qualities.

Not all hyperactive children grow out of their problems or learn to channel their restlessness with such conspicuous success. Left unchecked, hyperactive behaviour leads to behavioural problems at school and a pattern is set to go through into later life. In 1967 a study of fourteen hyperactive children first seen 25 years earlier showed three to be still hyperactive, four had been institutionalised as psychotic, two were retarded and unable to support themselves and of the eight who were self-supporting, one had been in prison and two had been in homes for the delinquent.

Meanwhile Feingold, paediatrician and allergist, came along, drew up a set of guidelines and gave his name to a 'diet' – though whether diet is the right word for something which is actually plain unadulterated food is debatable.

He claimed that food additives were responsible for the hyperactivity of between forty and fifty per cent of the hyperactive children he had seen in his practice, a statement that very soon had him battling to defend himself against attacks from the medical profession and the packaged food industry alike.

But the proof of his theory was in the eating, as increasing numbers of children given a daily diet free of all additives began to show by a radical change of behaviour.

Doctors and food manufacturers might pooh-pooh 'cranky' theories and 'kooky' diets, but desperate parents coping with uncontrollable children without any real understanding or help from the medical establishment were ready to try *anything*, including examining every label on every item of manufactured food to see if it contained one of the danger E numbers that identify chemical additives.

When Sally Bunday began what has become her life's work in 1977 she, too, was up against the same critics as Ben Feingold. Much has now changed for the simple reason that, however disbelieving the sceptics are about the extreme effects diet can have on behaviour, they can no longer ignore the living evidence.

Thousands of parents have written gratefully to HACSG to tell their experiences of remarkable change in their children after adopting an additive-free diet.

What in Ben Feingold's time could be regarded as an uncharacteristic sample of extremely disturbed children is now the reflection of the everyday findings of ordinary people, in their own homes and schools, dealing successfully with varying degrees of abnormal behaviour by following the Feingold rules.

Dr. Feingold identified as villains synthetic flavours, synthetic colours, some preservatives (hence the outcry from the junk food lobby) and certain natural foods said to contain salicylates (chemically related to aspirin) such as apples and cucumbers. He recommended an additive-free diet.

So which additives? It is now generally recognised that the E numbers cause the greatest problems. They identify colourings, preservatives, emulsifiers and flavourings and most of these (excluding the flavourings for some reason best known to EEC bureaucracy) must be recorded on the labels of all packaged food (as of July 1986).

Not all additives are harmful. Certain preservatives have been widely used for a century and many are of natural origin. Also on the bright side, food retailers, recognising growing public awareness, are actively co-operating to promote the development and sales of "safe" foods, particularly in what is generally regarded as children's lines. (Beware here, however, for there are many foods which form part of the family menu and as such are consumed by young children which are certainly suspect – sausages, processed meats, tinned peas and the like).

What the HACSG advocates is the elimination of synthetic chemical additives, colours, flavours and in some cases, for an initial period, also certain fruits and vegetables known to contain natural salicylates, the aspirin-like chemicals known to affect hyperactive children.

This means avoiding the obvious junk, examining with suspicion anything abnormally brightly coloured, especially the oranges and reds and yellows; asking yourself what actual FOOD is contained in the packet on offer. Food manufacturers believe that, like small children, we require everything to be paintbox bright. They believe the more garish the colours, the more tempted the customer, that as long as the product fulfils this criterion then the consumer is happy. Elsewhere in the world, manufacturers of processed food do not have this simplistic and somewhat cynical view of the consumer, neither are they permitted by law to use additives as freely as in the U.K. The Norwegian housewife may buy confident that her food is unadulterated by colourants . . . and the same goes for the Swedish customer with the exception of Cocktail Cherries and caviar, not food eaten in great quantities by small children.

So don't assume that "they" know best, read the labels on the packets.

So first cut out the suspect foods (having carefully scrutinised the labels and said a definite no to orange squash and lollies and almost anything called 'instant') and steer away from the packaged foods and towards the genuine foodstuffs, unprocessed, uncontaminated. At once this creates an overall improvement in the diet, with increased fibre, reduced fat and sugar and moderate rather than excessive salt.

Of course, the children will notice, and no doubt complain at suddenly being deprived of the sweets, lollies, crisps and endless sugary drinks they are virtually addicted too. Stay with it, the benefits are worth the initial struggle. Quite apart from the hyperactivity, there are tremendous benefits to be derived simply from establishing a healthy way of eating. Some people see a response within days, but it could take up to two weeks for the no-additive diet to produce results. If not, and if the child is still showing signs of allergy-type reaction (or if wheezing or a rash persist) then you know that additives are not the only source of the problem and you must look further for the cure – like the mother of Timothy . . .

TIMOTHY – "THREE OR FOUR DAYS ON EVENING PRIMROSE OIL AND MY HORRIBLE MONSTER SON TURNED INTO THE DEAREST LITTLE BOY"

"I cannot begin to tell you how very grateful my family and myself are for the wonderful work HACSG has done and the research you have carried out into diets and evening primrose oil. I truly believe we would all be in mental institutes by now if you had not helped us!

After hearing Sally Bunday talk in our village hall I bought Larkhill Labs oil of evening primrose and could see a noticeable difference in Timothy within a few days. His behaviour was fifty percent improved. When I got the papers on the dosage, I changed to Efamol evening primrose oil, which contains other oils as well.

Well . . . after about three or four days my horrible monster son turned into the dearest little boy! My husband and I were truly amazed. The terrible destruction and violence Timothy had shown completely stopped. I haven't had a black eye or cut lip since! (That was what he gave me six times a day during nappy change, when he'd kick and punch me). Within a couple of weeks Timothy was talking in sentences – he's two. The only word he used before was NO. He can now *play* with toys instead of stamping on them. His eyes used to be glazed and no amount of scolding or smacking had any effect. It all fell on deaf ears. I believe he is only now really seeing us and hearing us for the first time since he was born.

There had been a great improvement after putting him on an additive free diet, but with the introduction of the evening primrose oil Timothy's changes were quite traumatic, like welcoming a new child into our family and all the love we had always *wanted* to give but somehow it had been very difficult to be loving."

You will often hear it said (and frequently by doctors) that the person who eats a healthy, well-balanced diet has no need of vitamin pills. True, up to a point. In the case of adults the point being that someone who smokes and drinks and leads a stressful life needs to compensate for those essential nutrients which his or her lifestyle wastes, so vitamin supplements may be necessary.

Similarly, deficiencies are possible in children. As we have already discussed, their diet might be inadequate, but also they may have extra needs because of the requirements of rapid growth. "He'll outgrow his strength" older relatives used to say of the child who was shooting up too fast. Quite right too. The message here is that diet alone may not be sufficient to combat the hyperactive child's behavioural symptoms. He – or she – may be so deficient in vital minerals and vitamins that the nutrients in the improved natural diet cannot do their work.

These are the most common deficiencies:
IRON. a severe deficiency of iron can cause apathy, irritability and poor appetite, among other symptoms.
ZINC. People are just becoming aware that this is a much more common deficiency than was formerly understood. It is especially common in hyperactive children, can cause sleeplessness and lack of zinc affects the body's efficiency to absorb other essential nutrients.
VITAMINS B1 and B6. A high junk food diet means a virtual absence of these important vitamins – the lack can cause depression and learning problems, restlessness, night terrors, night sweats and similar neurotic symptoms.
MAGNESIUM. Children who drink a lot of cow's milk (consider the insatiable thirst of the hyperactive child) are shown to be magnesium-deficient. Disturbances include

muscle cramps, insomnia, tiredness and behaviour problems.

Studies carried out by the HACSG indicate that many hyperactive children thrive on supplements of evening primrose oil. This substance, in common with human breast milk, contains gamma-linolenic acid, a vital aid in helping hyperactive children to metabolise essential fatty acids. This vital substance, it is now known, also exists in blackcurrant seeds. Essential fatty acids are of paramount importance to health and cannot be manufactured by the body; they have to be taken in food. Natural foods like goat's milk and safflower oil contain linolenic acid, but in order to work efficiently in the body this must be converted into gamma-linolenic acid. Vitamins B, C and E and zinc do this work – if the child already has them in the body. A child like Timothy does not have them in sufficient quantity.

Evening primrose oil which contains gamma-linolenic acid should therefore be the perfect solution. However, in the controlled study carried out by HACSG, not *all* children improved noticeably. Those who did experienced dramatic and wholly encouraging improvements. Those who didn't were no worse off than they were before. There were no side effects.

The dosage was 2 to 3 grammes of oil daily, either by mouth or massaged into chest, stomach or thigh (but HACSG emphasise that you should not give evening primrose oil to children with epilepsy).

Evening primrose oil being a natural substance, is unlikely to do any harm and the HACSG tests demonstrated no adverse reactions even among children who did not appear to benefit favourably from the supplement. Should you overdo the dose the worst that could happen would be diarrhoea. Suggested dosages on cartons of evening primrose oil purchased from health shops are usually too high for young children, there are so many factors to consider other than the age of the child, so I would recommend writing to HACSG for further details.

In addition to supplements of evening primrose oil along with the Feingold diet, it is worth taking co-factors zinc, magnesium, B6, Niacin (B3) and Vitamin C which assists with the absorption and assimilation of the essential fatty acids and counteract the blocking effects of some food dyes and salicylates which could have slipped through the net.

Many hyperactive children seem to benefit enormously especially in the initial diagnosis and self-help programme, from a zinc supplement. It is not yet know how important zinc deficiency is, in relation to hyperactivity but it is known that zinc-impaired children can be jittery, irritable and inclined towards depression. The HACSG suggest 3.5 mg. of zinc to each ten pounds of body weight given as a supplement.

If you would like to monitor your child's zinc level before embarking on a zinc supplement, mineral analysis of hair is a good method for screening and involves snipping about an ounce of hair (taken from the back of the head and not in one chunk) and sending it for testing. To obtain a form for testing write to HACSG enclosing a s.a.e. There is too a simple taste test, devised by Professor Derek Bryce-Smith, the leading authority on Zinc, and a commercial form of this test is available from Nature's Best (see page 86).

Possibly this is all beginning to sound like very hard work. Not only that, but nobody wants to be labelled some sort of health freak, unrealistically obsessed with endless discussions on food and little Billy's anti-social behaviour. In practice however, the benefits as you go along are so profound that not only are you eager to learn more, you actually have more energy and enthusiasm to tackle each step . . . indeed more energy and enthusiasm for *life*.

To watch a child you could have strangled, a child you were growing to dislike, become transformed into normal is reward enough and is the spur to press on with the challenge if it appears there are still areas left to look into.

So begin by removing the obvious junk. Eat only whole food. Cut out all sweets, cakes, white bread, sugary drinks. Let nature do its work. Then, if you think there is a need, try *judicious* use of supplements like evening primrose oil.

To try a short cut by feeding supplements to someone on a junk diet is a total waste of time and money.

Many readers, having come this far, may have seen a 'snapshot' likeness to their own child in Jennifer, David or Timothy and will see their way out of Sugarland. But some will find that an additive-free diet and even vitamin or mineral supplements do not provide the whole answer. Michael was a boy with a problem like that . . .

MICHAEL – "WITHIN MINUTES HIS EYES STARTED TO GO VERY RED AND SORE"

"My son has been on the Feingold diet now for eight weeks with very good results. I thought you might be interested to know that the other day, for the first time, he started to scrape some new potatoes. Within minutes his eyes started to go very red and sore and he had to stop what he was doing. A few days later, out shopping, we were in the stationery department and he was going around smelling the rubbers (you know the type). Suddenly the redness and soreness appeared around his eyes again.

He has been so well since putting him on the Feingold diet. He used to have quite bad nosebleeds before and they stopped completely. Except once, when we broke the diet with an apple and an asprin and he had two nosebleeds in the same week."

Michael was having an allergic reaction either to the chemical residues remaining on the potato skins or to the salicylates contained in the potatoes – the same salicylates as are present in apples and aspirin. Similar chemicals are used in rubbers, pens and felt tips and you will remember that Jennifer reacted wildly whenever she sucked a felt tip pen. Nosebleeds are another symptom the hyperactive child is prone to, caused by food and chemical sensitivity.

Whilst additives and colourings account for a huge proportion of hyperactive problems (and to eliminate these from your family's day-to-day food intake can do no harm whatsoever, even if so doing does not cure the hyperactivity) there are other causes of disturbed behaviour, such as food allergy.

We all know about allergies, don't we?. We know people who are allergic to mussels or lobster, grapefruit or chocolate. People can be allergic to deodorant, soap powder, furniture polish. Every June thousands of school examination candidates are at their lowest ebb because of hay fever. Allergy isn't a new illness, but its prevalence is increasing – as do the numbers of substances capable of causing the sensitive reaction.

The hyperactive child starts out being more sensitive than most, more vulnerable to becoming allergic to something. Since not all children are prone to allergies, nor seriously adversely affected by additives and some salicylates, then there must be something about the hyperactive child that sets him apart.

We know that it has to do with the body's immune system, that delicate monitoring complex. We know that a substance called essential fatty acid is required before the body can make the prostaglandins which control the immune system, and that some people do not have these essential fatty acids, and we as yet do not know why some people are unable to manufacture EFAs. The first six months of life are the crucial time, when a baby's immune system is being developed.

Perhaps his vulnerability to becoming hyperactive was established in the womb (many HACSG mothers recall abnormally energetic kicking and moving during the pregnancy) and too there are other factors which match up. Perhaps he was born deficient in zinc or other essential nutrients needed to produce the enzymes which ensure food is correctly metabolised, and also for the correct functioning of the adrenal gland. If his mother had a low level of nutrition during pregnancy, if she smoked then, if she was taking the contraceptive pill to within six months of conception, the new baby will be inclined to be allergy-prone. Our baby's chances are further increased if he comes from a family with a history of allergies... asthma for instance.

The Greeks knew that certain foods were poison to certain people and for generations wise adults have observed for themselves that some people should simply avoid specific foods, but until only a few years ago anyone talking of food allergy as a significant cause of illness and behavioural problems had a hard time convincing the non-believers. Today clinical and academic proof is incontrovertible. The job is now down to identifying the culprit allergen in individual cases and establishing the degree of reaction.

Experience has shown that cow's milk, cow's milk products, wheat, chocolate, citrus fruits and fruits containing salicylates are the commonest culprits in allergies. Solvents (as present in aerosol sprays, coloured felt tipped pens and cleaning fluids) can be extremely potent allergenic substances.

Some children have an allergic reaction to medication, due either to the drugs themselves or the additives used to colour the medicine. A product specifically designed to encourage children to clean their teeth, by staining the plaque and thus showing it up, is somewhat illogically coloured with Erythrosine, the dreaded E127.

If a mother suspects medication of having a bad effect on her child, then she should immediately take this up with her doctor. If the doctor feels that the symptoms cannot be attributed to the drug itself, then she should ask to be prescribed for a form that has no added colour. If that fails, it is worth discussing the problem with the pharmacist, who may be able to suggest a more suitable form of the drug.

Removing the junk element in the diet will have enormously beneficial results, but it will not automatically deal with a specific allergy. So if eliminating additives and maintaining a good whole food diet for several weeks does not help your hyperactive child or if some symptoms of the hyperactivity still persist, then you should be alerted to the possibility of allergy and you need to look more carefully at the daily food intake.

Start by keeping a day-to-day log of everything the child eats, with a second column recording behaviour. Are certain symptoms apparent after a particular food has been eaten?

If this doesn't answer the question, then the next step is some type of elimination diet. By excluding one type of staple food at a time and recording behaviour alongside, you set out to track down which part of the basic diet is causing the allergic reaction. It could be milk or cereals (possibly activated if the child was weaned on to cereals too early), or citrus allergy to early orange juice. Symptoms would have been present when the offending food was first taken and most mothers will be able to recall bad bouts of diarrhoea and restlessness, a baby who was difficult to settle at night. I heard of one three-year-old whose parents had their first night's sleep in three years when cow's milk was removed from her diet (and, in her case, replaced with soya). The detective work had paid off.

Don't attempt an elimination diet if the child is underweight or has been off his or her food for some time without first providing a nutritional supplement and an improved whole food diet. It is, of course, perfectly safe and positively helpful to eliminate at any time – preferably straight away – additives, colourings, preservatives, salicylates and sugar and refined carbohydrates such as biscuits, cakes, sweets.

No harm can be done by removing dairy produce from the child's food for up to two weeks, if this is the "suspect", and you will receive your answer quite promptly. However, to try a more sophisticated elimination diet could be risky. So much depends on the age, health and general wellbeing of the child.

There are tried and tested methods of excluding various

foods, one at a time, then reintroducing to test for response which in the case of persistent allergy symptoms are undertaken. However, it is Sally Bunday's belief that elimination diets should only be carried out under medical supervision.

So far I have been instancing cases of seriously disturbed children who would be diagnosed hyperactive. But additive-reaction can affect 'ordinary' children in a less dramatic way, as the Coopers of Southampton demonstrate . . .

THE COOPERS – "JUST AN ORDINARY FAMILY – NOT HYPERACTIVITY, BUT REACTING BADLY"

"Last year while on our holiday it suddenly dawned on my husband that the drinks we were treating our children to in cafes and tavernas were causing them to change from friendly, happy children into unreasonable, anti-social, anti-everything beings, almost as if possessed by devils. The worst offender was Coca Cola. One drink and about 3-4 minutes later the change was evident.

We now follow a diet free from colourants (especially EFA) and have cut out fizzy drinks. Our children, age 6 and 7 years, have accepted this and realise that the banned foods and drinks change them. (However, whilst under the influence you can neither reason with them nor expect them to understand). My son needs only a few crisps, a lolly, a drink, to bring about this almost schizophrenic change, making him unmanageable. My daughter reacts by being unable to keep still.

I feel very bitter that their pre-school years at home were a trial for me and not as happy as they should have been for them as a result of these unnecessary additives. I now have a one-month-old son who is breast-fed and will NOT be given the usual fish fingers, processed peas, orange squash, etc. which, due to my ignorance, I fed my other children. The result will be interesting."

Far more children are affected by chemicals in their bodies than just those seen to be hyperactive. Like the Cooper children, they may react sporadically in a cranky, uncharacteristic way to certain highly chemical foods. Or, if the diet is regularly inadequate or additive-high, they may suffer from poor concentration and tiredness, be easily upset and experience learning difficulties. There could be as many as one in four children in this category.

Inadequate diet, junk food and irregular eating can lead to hypoglycaemia, or low blood sugar, another cause of hyperactivity. If too much insulin is produced too much sugar is driven into the cells, thus reducing the blood sugar to too low a level. The effect of this is to rob the brain cells of vital glucose which the brain needs for normal functioning. Hence many of the symptoms of hypoglycaemia – irritability, headaches, behaviour problems and moodiness. In other words what we all know, a hungry child is a fractious child. Eating a bar of chocolate, something "sweet" has the opposite effect to that required, the refined sugar overloads the unfortunate pancreas and makes matters worse. Thus in the potentially hyperactive child, hypoglycaemia is yet another trigger and constant injections of refined carbohydrates – sugary foods, biscuits, synthetic snacks causes hypoglycaemia.

I once spent an interesting interlude with Sally Bunday, in which we calculated the likely food intake over the previous twenty-four hours of a particularly ugly bunch of soccer hooligans who had run riot in an orgy of damage and violence. The match was played on a Saturday afternoon and the 'away' fans had in many cases started their journey the previous evening. It wasn't difficult to work out what they'd eaten – crisps, bars of chocolate, beers and cokes, possibly processed pies, at the best hot dogs. Excluding those among them actually allergic to the junk content, the rest would be in a state of hypoglycaemia, highly inflammatory, like a bomb waiting to explode.

Teachers will tell you they can spot the child who has come to school without a decent breakfast, because of his poor performance and low concentration. By the same token, staying up late at night glued to the television is not conducive to getting out of bed early enough the following morning to allow for a proper whole food breakfast. Children who rush out of the house on an empty stomach, with lunch money which they spend in the sweet shop, are perpetuating possible hypoglycaemia. The current style in school catering offering 'choice' means that children with bad eating habits simply perpetuate those habits, reaching for the chips in preference to the salad, the processed 'fruit' pie in preference to the fresh fruit.

You will have noticed the references to slow speech or no speech in the stories of hyperactive children that their mothers have been telling. A link between chemical food additives and poor speech development has long been suspected but like so many areas of research into hyperactivity and related symptoms, has depended more on the evidence of experience from parents than on clinical surveys.

Recently Sally Bunday heard from a speech therapist working almost exclusively with children.

"I have been delighted to see the almost immediate change in one of my patient's behaviour and language development as a result of being put on a diet free from preservatives and colourings.

"I understand that delayed speech and language development can sometimes be symptomatic of allergy towards these additives and feel that any information you could provide may be of benefit towards my work."

Sally had received many reports from parents telling of their child's speech improvement on the HASCG diet, but to have such a letter from an expert was a real bonus. Tartrazine, the substance denoted by a dreaded E number (E102) is known to cause odema or swelling of the middle ear, which could possibly link up with speech difficulties.

A family whose 8-year-old son had suffered from an ear infection since he was three were told that there was little that could be done, although he had had several operations to try to cure the problem. A friend read in a HACSG newsletter of the link between diet and childhood diseases, passed on the information and the family implemented an additive-free diet at once, with dramatic results. The boy now has complete hearing in both ears.

One doctor in Kent hands out a three-page advice document to patients in despair over behaviour-disturbed youngsters, exhorting them to "get back to preparing and cooking food the way Granny used to. The main difficulty for the busy parent is that more time needs to be taken selecting and preparing food. But the rewards gained will far outweigh the disadvantages, and you'll soon adapt to and enjoy the new style of living, to the benefit of the whole family."

A concerned (and extremely tactful) Gloucestershire grandmother wrote the following letter to Sally Bunday.

"A while back you sent me your literature on diets for 'wild' children and I left it where my distraught daughter would find it. She did, and has been feeding her three little terrors accordingly. I cannot tell you how wonderfully the diet, or careful shopping and feeding have changed the whole life of that little family. My daughter has been able to go back to her old job, even if only for one day a week. We had all three children to stay for last half-term on their own without parents and it was a happy, lovely week. I cannot thank you enough for the magic transformation of my three grandsons, aged 8, 6 and 3."

This granny certainly knew best. She knew something was wrong and she managed to give advice without giving offence. She has her reward in seeing the happiness and love grow in her daughter's family, and the strengthening of their security.

Have we forgotten the sound common-sense that granny always knew instinctively? At least one organizer of the

HACSG self-help counselling sessions tells her mothers: "We've got to get back to how granny used to cook. Simple food. You actually save money in the long run."

Grannies didn't believe in wasting money on rubbish. You could argue that in their day grannies didn't have the vast amounts of rubbishy, chemical-laden foods to choose from. Today, sadly, the abundance of choice has resulted in vast numbers of the population being virtually under-nourished.

The Coopers are an ordinary family with a manageable problem. Given the HACSG information, they can cope very well. But family life is changing today and some parents have to cope in a less supportive environment. Some have to cope alone, like Stephen's mother . . .

STEPHEN'S MOTHER: "A LONE PARENT – AN IMPOSSIBLE BURDEN".

"After two years of absolute hell I was driven to calling the Samaritans and, by sheer chance (or a helpful guardian angel), I called at a time when the gentleman on duty had once had a hyperactive grandchild. He was able to send me a copy of the HACGS diet sheet and within 24 hours I *knew* it was going to work.

Now, three weeks later, I am able to take my son out and know he will behave almost normally whereas before the diet I had to keep trips out of the house to a minimum and on essential food shopping trips I had to streak round in double quick time before he made an exhibition of himself.

Many, many time I've come home and cried buckets after unkind comments from passers-by and shop-keepers about him needing a good spanking. Believe me, I have spanked him till I've bruised him, with absolutely no results.

When he's been on a particularly bad spell, there have been days when all I've had to eat has been a bowl of porridge because I literally didn't dare go to the shops. (This whilst breast-feeding a younger child, too).

I am a lone parent living on an estate miles from town so this has made the situation worse. The only help I had from my health visitor – though I've been visiting the clinic regularly both with the boy and later with my baby girl – was that she found a day nursery place for me at a nursery on the other side of town. I daren't use buses and had to walk everywhere. To get there for 9.30 a.m. I would have had to leave home by

7.30 a.m. Also the fee was £1.50 per morning and I live on Social Security, so £7.50 a week was out of the question. The only other advice from her was a suggestion that I should have Stephen adopted if it got too much for me.

She could arrange it!

There was never any mention of hyperactiveness until the telephone Samaritan recognised the similarity to his own grandchild and helped me.

It grieves me to think that for two years I have lived like a prisoner, not able to go out and not able to have anybody to the house because I was ashamed of Stephen. I thought he was mental. Indeed at times I doubted my own sanity, too – and all the time this diet was available and nobody put me on to it.

During the last year my son had made no progress. He seems to have regressed in some things – his speaking is worse now then when he was small. (Incidentally he was a very bright and forward baby. He said recognisable words at 5½ months old). His legs seem to have gone weak; he stumbles and falls frequently. His appetite is now poor. Is this the case with hyperactive children and will he now catch up on the learning time he appears to have lost?

Secondly, now he has started to slow down – and therefore I am slowing down too, he appears to have gone to the other extreme. He has gone from hardly sleeping at all to having a sleep lasting three and a half hours each day plus a full night. Is this, as I surmise, a healing reaction of some sort? Does it always happen and how long will this phase last? I know how he feels. I had to be uptight to keep up with him and now I can finally relax and unwind I feel like a limp rag doll. The housework has been half done for such a long time that another few weeks won't hurt. I feel we both need to convalesce.

But I also feel I may have done him some psychological harm with the terrible things I have said to him when I've lost my temper in the past. That's something only time will tell and I can't put that right, regrettably. In the meantime any advice you can give me of any sort would be gratefully received and put to use.

I will say again that I thank you from the bottom of my heart for the help that your diet sheet has been to me. I'm not exaggerating when I say that it's probably been a life saver. I doubt if I could have taken much more without cracking up and doing something silly."

Sally Bunday was able to reassure the mother.

"The regression in development is quite common. The stumbling and falling and poor appetite can be linked to shortages of important minerals and too much of some toxic ones, such as lead and copper. The sleeping could be a form of healing and, depending on age, can be quite normal. Most toddlers need lots of sleep. Don't forget you have all been living at such a high pitch for ages. You do need to catch up.

"Don't worry about what you have said in the past. We all say horrid things, but the children don't worry as much as we do – at least, I hope that is the case."

The past two decades have seen many changes in traditional family life. One in eight families is now a one-parent family. The way we live within the family group has changed – ask a friend to list the changes she is aware of; it is endlessly fascinating. Patterns of family eating have changed dramatically too. In place of the family meal we have developed a habit of eating on the wing, numerous snacks instead of the two or three traditional meals of the day. These snacks are invariably 'convenience' – bags of crisps, bars of chocolate, flaccid sandwiches, plastic wrapped, in station kiosks.

Instead of an evening meal around the kitchen table it's more likely to be TV dinner from a packet on your lap or a takeaway additive-laden burger. Convenience foods suit our new lifestyle. Except that what is called 'convenience' is very often junk.

Problems of bad housing and unemployment impose an additional burden on the family. A hyperactive child adds to the sum total of despair or possibly is hyperactive because of environmental difficulties. It's a chicken and egg situation. One doctor working in the field says, "Diet and lifestyle go together. And it isn't always among the materially disadvantaged that one sees severe tension. Occasionally a child is presented as hyperactive, has all the symptoms, then you observe the parents in the home, see two people obsessed with keeping everything neat and tidy, tense and complaining about their naughty child, touchy and impatient. You can see that there is an allergy but it is only part of the child's problem, that what he desperately needs is to be reassured that his parents want him. Sometimes his awful behaviour is the only way he can guarantee their undivided attention.

"By the same token the child from a family where he is turned out to play aged two and allowed to roam in the street all day until bedtime, – well, putting him on a whole food diet, even assuming the parental co-operation was there, isn't going to alter appreciably his behavioural problems at a later stage."

Education officials in Birmingham recently revealed that more than 60,000 children (around one-third of their school population) had serious behavioural problems, including poor concentration, serious aggression towards their fellow classmates, violence, fatigue – a familiar list to those who work with hyperactivity. Their report stated: "Nearly all the children affected were from low-income families, a large number brought up by single parents . . . a home lifestyle of late-night videos and junk food."

Although there has (at time of writing) been no official National Health Service funded investigation into hyperactivity, an eminent medical team from the Department of Immunology and Child Psychiatry, Great Ormond Street Hospital, London, carried out a study into the behaviour of 76 selected hyperactive children and pronounced that "colourants and preservatives were the commonest substances that provoked abnormal behaviour in our patients . . ."

Dr. Ian Menzies of Dundee Infirmary's Children and Young People's Psychiatric Unit, says: "We know of children responding to the diet and nutritional approach who otherwise were heading for a place in a special school, at a cost to the taxpayer of around ten thousand pounds a year. It makes sense to try easy remedies first. Sadly, nutrition is not as yet a subject that figures large in the training of the medical practitioner."

In the field of child psychiatry, specialists are taking a close look at food as a contributory factor in behaviour. Dr. John Simons, a London practitioner, maintains: "If it became part of the process that every child psychiatric patient was screened for diet, both for food intolerance and for chemical sensitivity, then we would be making huge inroads into the behavioural problems of children. For too long we have omitted to consider the effect that large doses of chemicals introduced through food to a child's delicate metabolism can have."

And a doctor working in general practice in Somerset wrote to HACSG to say:

"I deal almost weekly with young mothers presenting children with either borderline or fully developed symptoms of hyperactivity. I am finding the commonest presented problem is sleep disturbance and often this is within the first few weeks after birth.

"Some of my patients are much longer-suffering and finally drag themselves to see us by the time their child is about to start school. The sleep deprivation experienced by the parents is, I am sure, a fundamental factor in a number of cases of marital disharmony and, what is more, seems to be harming their relationship with their own children."

As the National Marriage Guidance Council says:

"Serious disability affects the whole family and imposes a severe burden on the marriage and hyperactivity is, of course, a very serious disability. It is a double-edged thing this, isn't it? If the marriage is very strong, very established, it will help to get parents through the problem of the sick child. If it isn't strong of its own accord, the strain will prove too much. In our experience this is a familiar recurring feature of marriage breakdown."

The link between hyperactivity and baby battering is also significant and it is not difficult to see why. Take one endlessly demanding, aggressive, destructive child who, whatever his age, seems incapable of the slightest co-operation and a mother driven to desperation by her own helplessness and lack of sleep (and possibly lack, too, of another supportive adult) and it doesn't take much imagination to see how a small strategically-administered slap becomes a violent, uncontrolled thump.

Take an angry father on the dole 'banged up inside four walls' and an uncontrollably active, actively disobedient child and you can recognise the danger.

The NSPCC, with its dramatic and horrifying 42% increase in cases in 1987, sees hyperactivity in the child as a significant factor in child abuse.

The Society's new system of operating in teams, so that each case is approached initially on a wider basis, enables the combined skills of, say, doctor, child psychiatrist, local playgroup, to pitch in with a massive back up. However, they admit: "It would be useful if we had a national overview on hyperactivity. We are still finding out about it, in the same way that we are still finding out about child abuse."

The British Association of Social Workers "don't see it as an issue that's high profile". Sally Bunday's experience would contradict that, and parents who feel themselves on the edge of violence will find understanding, help and advice with the HACSG.

LETTERS TO SALLY BUNDAY.

The greatest help to parents demoralised by their failure to get anywhere with a hyperactive child is often the simple realisation that there are others like themselves. Talking it over, sharing experiences, discussing the possibilities with other parents, somehow makes it easier to try a fresh start with hope and determination.

For this reason I am including a further selection of correspondence from the files of the HACSG. This may be where you will come face to face with your own Nellie Beast – or your own weary despair – and, recognising a fellow sufferer, see your own way forward.

The HACSG has 10,000 members, all dedicated to helping others, and has responded to requests for information from close to 100,000. Through Sally Bunday's intervention one mother has been saved from having her children taken into care. A responsive social worker helped the mother establish that all three are hyperactive and, with carefully monitored food, all three are now responding and being rehabilitated in their own home.

DAMON'S STORY "I often felt: one day I'll hit him so hard I'll kill him"

Life with Damon was sheer hell. "So awful that I was not accepted by any friends. There was never a night when he slept longer than an hour – my husband and I took it in turns to be with him. He screamed, he was destructive, he couldn't eat a proper meal, he was intolerable. He ruined our lives because nobody wanted to know us.

"We couldn't let him cry himself into too much of a tantrum because it would bring on an asthma attack. Even when he was ill and needed to go into hospital, they couldn't keep him in very long because they couldn't cope with him. That was my one consolation. At least they couldn't manage any better, it wasn't all my fault. I used to smack him very hard. I admit I made marks. I often felt: "One day I'll hit him so hard I'll kill him".

"One Saturday morning my husband took over and I was given time off to go to the hairdresser. I sat down in the chair, picked up a magazine and, flicking through, read a small piece about the Feingold diet. It was like a religious coversion. I jumped out of the chair, flung off the gown and rushed home. I knew this had to be the answer. Within four days Damon had made a miraculous recovery and soon became a normal, happy, loving little two-year-old.

"He is now six and I monitor everything he eats. If he's invited to a friend he takes his own food unless the mother is one of us, reads the packet labels! We had a small accident a few weeks ago. "Two days of irritability and aggressiveness. By luck I happened to spot the offending Tartrazine. In the last place I expected to find it – a packet of breakfast cereal someone had given us. I threw it out at once."

PETER: "Guinea pig in a homeopathic cure"

"A year ago I discovered that my younger son had an allergy to Tartrazine and was hyperactive. I have since been prompted to contact you by the paediatrician at our local hospital, who is using my son as a 'guinea pig' in a homeopathic cure.

"First perhaps I should give you the history of my child. He was born by Caesarian Section at almost full term, 9 lb. in weight with no problems. For the first three months he was very placid but bright with no problems. At about 3½ months I began to notice he was very windy. He began having screaming fits and was not sleeping so well. At 5½ months I had him checked at the baby clinic but was told he had colic. My problems from then on until he was eighteen months old got worse.

"The symptoms he suffered were bouts of screaming, two-three hours, particularly at night. Severe rash and irritation around his middle. Not sleeping in the day and very little at night – no more than three hours at a stretch. Unquenchable thirst and insatiable appetite. Destructive behaviour. Permanent frown on forehead. During the night when his screaming fits were over he would play until he was exhausted.

"During this time it never occurred to me that he could be classed as hyperactive because he is exceptionally bright. He walked at 12 months, not taking tottering steps but walking very confidently. He crawled at 5½ months. At 12 months he began to talk, learning one new word a day for the first week, about three a day for the next two weeks and after that I lost count. "Much of his vocabulary was developed during our many sleepless nights when he seemed at his most receptive. His manual dexterity was also very good. His speech was very clear and he would not be daunted by long words. At 15 months he attempted to say "procrastinating'! Before he was two years old he could use a knife and fork. He was not taught. At his fifteen months development assessment he could have done his 2½-year one, but he was not always co-operative.

"As soon as I eliminated Tartrazine from his diet he behaviour changed dramatically. Within twenty-four hours he slept for ten hours and within four days was sleeping twelve to thirteen hours a night. He started eating much less and drinking only moderate amounts. Within a month his appearance changed. He began to look happy, lost the heavy look in his eyes and his usually white face became pink and healthy looking. His behaviour changed, too, and he no longer had tantrums or destroyed things.

"From the discovery of Tartrazine I was very careful with his diet. I gave him only fresh food – meat and vegetables, home-made cakes, Rich Tea biscuits, eggs. All sweets, junk food and convenience foods were banned. I had the odd slip-up when other people gave him food or sweets without my knowledge. I found educating some people, particularly grandparents, very difficult. I had a reasonably clear six months with Peter and then I began to get sleepless nights again, usually losing about three hours a night when he would shout out, scream, talk. I began to realise he was hallucinating.

"In December 1983, after a chance meeting with the consultant paediatrician at our local hospital, I discovered that Peter was allergic to blackcurrant jam. This made me go back to the Feingold diet.

"It seems that Peter is allergic to blackcurrants, red currants, gooseberries, oranges and other citrus fruits. He reacts very badly to Double Gloucester cheese and Cheddar. Vanillin is another allergy and I think vanilla – but vanilla essence has colouring in also. Silver Spoon Golden Syrup, Aspirin and smoked mackerel bring bad reactions. I haven't tried other smoked fish.

"Peter is now being seen by the pediatrician at Bronglais Hospital, Aberystwyth, and we are now trying homeopathic treatment of the Tartrazine and of Aspirin."

Homeopathic remedies for hyperactivity are being examined. The view of the HACSG is: "We are always concerned when children receive Homeopathic remedies for food additives because it means that the additive is still being taken into the body and could do some harm which has not yet been investigated. Our advice is to avoid the chemicals completely, but to have a homeopathic remedy for the allergy if it is basic foods and fruits which are nourishing – unlike additives which are on the whole chemicals and have no nutritional value."

KEIRON: "A very sad, tearful little boy"

"Keiron is my grandson. Until he was five years old I lived quite near so I did see a lot of him as a baby. Keiron had had a very sad and unhappy life. I know that on two occasions, at 4 months and 7 months, I saw bad bruises on his face and head which his mother admitted she had done by hitting him because he would not stop crying. I know I should have reported this, but I did not want my little grandson put into care, so I just had him as often as I could.

"When Keiron was five we moved away and ten days later his father left his mother. I will never know which upset Keiron most, his grandparents leaving or his father, but he was very upset and lost a lot of weight and became a very sad, tearful little boy.

"His parents were divorced and both married a second time. His mother had custody of Keiron; his father could not as the woman he married would not have the child.

"His stepfather was unkind to Keiron and often beat him. It would be about two years ago this month that Keiron began to phone once or twice a week, often sobbing and crying and saying how unhappy he was and could he come and live with grandad and me, (Grandad has since passed away) just for five years until he left school. In his little mind he didn't think he would need a home when he had left school. It was very upsetting and I spoke to his mother and asked what was going on and why Keiron was so unhappy. I was told "You can have him". I also spoke to his father. He told me Keiron was very unhappy but he couldn't have him to live with him. So, you see, neither his mother nor father wanted him.

"Two years ago he came to live with me and started at middle school. Then he started continual chattering and upsetting the whole class, doing anything to be taken notice of. He cannot get on with children of his own age group; he prefers to be with younger children. Last September he went to the senior school and again the same trouble started. Now he brings a report home each day for me to sign and the behaviour is very poor with little concentration in any lesson.

"At home he is very hard to manage, always wanting his own way and getting into bad tempers if he cannot have what he wants. It's very hard to get him to bed. I did take Keiron to the Child Guidance Clinic last year, but this was not very helpful. They seemed to think Keiron was right to want his own way and I should let him have it if he was happy. I must just put up with his tantrums – but at 70 years of age, it's not so easy.

"I have had no real advice or help with Keiron. I do not know where to take him. I don't think it is much good taking him to the GP as Keiron is not ill in himself. So where do I go for help?

"I will try the died – I expect he will make a fuss, but if there is no other food in the house he will have to eat it or go hungry – not for long, he is very fond of his food. I would be grateful for any advice you can give me. I feel so alone and helpless with Keiron and his tantrums at home and school and bringing a child up on a pension is not easy by any means without having extra troubles to content with."

MARK: "Visions of a raging delinquent by the time he reached his teens"

"Mark was orphaned at the age of two, when his mother died. He was taken into a children's home where he spent a great deal of the time screaming. This went on for several months. When we adopted him at the age of four he was labelled a 'disturbed child' and his medical record stated that he might be hyperactive. It is difficult to describe now what he was like at that time, but I will try.

"He talked almost non-stop even when alone. He slept very little and was absolutely uncontrollable in his behaviour. At times he would appear to go berserk. He could not relate to other children as he tended to be too silly and uncontrolled in his behaviour or at times aggressive. He could not sit still, with the result that he was continually breaking things or, if nothing was to hand, he would tear the skin off his fingers and toes (in bed) until they were raw.

"When he went to school, the matter became far worse, as he no longer had the undivided attention of one adult for the greater part of the day. He could not keep still or keep quiet long enough to do any work at all and term after term he brought home empty books. He was extremely disruptive and a nastier side to his character appeared to be developing.

"He could not learn to read at school, but fortunately at that time he had an understanding teacher who suggested that I taught him to read at home, where he would not be distracted. Within two days he was reading fluently and by the time he was seven he had a reading age of thirteen. Because of his behaviour problems we transferred him to a private school where he was made to work, although his behaviour continued to be disruptive and anti-social, due largely to his inability to stay in one place or to stop talking.

"By this time he was aware of his problems and was becoming easily upset, feeling he was expected to be able to control himself, but finding that he could not. Even when he was four he had complained to us that his head was 'buzzing' that it was 'full of too many thoughts' and that he couldn't sleep because his head wouldn't let him.

"When he was eight we heard mention of the HACSG on Woman's Hour on the radio. I made a note of the address and wondered vaguely whether it would be worth writing for help. In the end I did and was sent the 'diet' sheets. I was extremely sceptical but willing at that time to try anything as I had visions of Mark becoming a raging delinquent by the time he reached his teens.

"After two weeks on the diet the most noticeable thing was that he stopped fidgeting with his fingers and managed to sit still for the first time ever. After 6 weeks he was sleeping normally and without any of the bad dreams he had been used to. It became easier for him to control his own behaviour so that he tended to be a disruptive influence only when he was upset and not as a general rule. He became less confused and vague and the better side of his nature made its appearance, showing him to be highly sensitive, thoughtful, generous and extremely loving – all qualities that had been disguised for so long.

"He has been on the diet for over two years now and while he is still a very lively boy and apt still to be in trouble in the classroom, there is little that he cannot put right himself and as long as he has plenty to occupy him he is no problem.

"Lest anyone should think that he has outgrown his hyperactivity and that the diet is coincidental to this, I would say that he has only to have, say, a highly coloured sweet from a friend at school for me to recognise immediately the signs – a distracted wild look in his eyes, a careless attitude to things, a jerkiness of manner and irresponsible and unreliable behaviour. All sure signs to me that were it not for the diet, my earlier fears would have proved to have been well founded."

SIMON: "Thank you for the child I should have had from the start"

"How can I describe my joy, my wonderment and my gratitude for Simon's cure? He had become sheer murder to live with. I had reached desperation point with my eighth fire-lighting episode and had a really bad fire round the chimney breast when I phoned one of the Hyperactive Children's Support Group volunteers and was told about the diet.

"Prior to this solution Simon had gradually become worse and worse as the years had gone by. I think now I can pinpoint the beginning to his starting on white baby cereals. He seemed to be always moving his limbs, unable to remain still even for a short while.

"While toddling he was into everything and I just could

not keep up with his energy and destructiveness. For a rest I used to put him in his cot, but his leaping up and down eventually broke the bottom – besides, he was a big boy and strong for his age. He never seemed to learn what was naughty and what was good. I'd scold him for something and in a couple of hours he was doing the same thing again.

"What made it worse for me was the fact that my ex-husband became a baby batterer. Eventually my marriage broke up because of it. I love children and could not stand to see Simon bruised or severely punished any more, in spite of trying to see my husband's point of view.

"Now – for the first time in my life I know peace. Simon is 7 years old now and has been on the Feingold 'diet' for approximately 7 months. He is obedient and doesn't quarrel with what I say all the time. He will now be 'normally' naughty occasionally and not abnormally frequently.

"He is not violent to me or his sister or others.

"He is no longer unmanageable at school. He can concentrate, so is enjoying learning to read and he can speak well now. He is able to enjoy other children for the first time. In the past, although he was friendly for a while, he'd quickly put others off by turning nasty for no reason.

"When I was first told about the diet and sent for the diet sheet I was desperate and determined to try anything, as I had no solution to his problems from doctors, psychiatrists or social workers. They were just as mystified as I was. I decided to be drastic and to modify his likes in food to the way they should be to suit the diet. I also decided to try to observe the effects as dispassionately as possible, as I would a casualty's symptoms in my St. John Ambulance work. I found, lo and behold, it did work. By the end of the first week he seemed much improved and has continued to be so.

"All I can say is a big thank you to all the members of the HACSG and a big thank you to Dr. Feingold and other doctors involved with this work. Thank you for the child I should have had from the start but didn't until now."

BENJAMIN: "He's a different child – but how do you heal his mind?"

"Benjamin is now a loving, gentle, caring 10-year-old. His temper is under control. He hasn't had a rage for more than a year, the occasional outburst being quickly controlled by his counting to ten. He stays within the classroom and does *some* work. (We still hope for improvement here). His sleep is more peaceful and longer. He eats much, much less, perhaps a third less than before. We can talk to him and he responds.

"He has his lapses. What ten-year-old wouldn't give in to the occasional temptation of junk food or sweets when out?. We never tell him off. He knows himself by the lack of control over his body. He comments on it himself and says he will try harder. These lapses serve to remind us of the son we had for so long.

"Thank God for the diet. Thank God for your association. It's time people realised just what damage is being done to our next generation. People still think that it's 'cranky'. I still get the odd funny look from people who didn't know Benjamin before. My friends and family are 100% convinced. They have seen the miracle.

"What I would say is this. Yes, the diet works. Yes, Benjamin is a different child. But how do you heal his mind? For his formative years he has been told he was 'naughty', 'dim', 'a trouble-maker'. He said to me recently, 'I can't be an engineer like Dad because I have no brain. I will have to dig holes in roads'. I know children can be very cruel but this has scarred his mind and no amount of contradiction from us will alter this state of mind. It's his peer group that counts and he recalls only too vividly what other children said of him and to him.

"I worry that we are going to have a lot of mentally damaged adults in the future."

JAMIE

Jamie's mother writes:

"This is a letter which is so lovely to be able to write. Last year I wrote and told you all about our little foster son Jamie, who had been brain damaged due to a battering by his parents and was, to say the very least, extremely difficult! Although, as I told you, we had very great support from doctors and psychologists nothing seemed to have helped. So armed with the diet and an open mind we felt we had nothing to lose and would try anything to help Jamie. Both the neurosurgeon and our paediatrician gave us support, his school teacher as usual was marvellous. He is still at a diagnostic unit, which only has ten children in the class, with a teacher, nursery nurse and helpers, so every child is a somebody and the staff all want them to do well. His food and drinks at school are all closely watched.

"We started to diet properly in October and are delighted with the results, he is calmer, not so aggressive and generally much easier to live with; not always crying and shouting. Night times too things have settled down. He is still a night owl but more content to go in the lounge and play, not continually crying and calling. We still lock all other doors and windows for his own safety. The goods which seem to cause the problems are orange squash and anything with colour; his favourite fish fingers, sausages, chocolate, these are just a few, also his medicine for headaches – Calpol. Our doctor has subsequently changed this for soluble panadol, after first finding out about Calpol and its added colour.

"(One thing that occurs to me is that possibly Jamie had his problems before he was battered and that only added injury).

"Our other marvellous news is that Jamie's adoption went through on the 20th of last month so now we have a very special son, our little treasure."

THE PROBLEMS OF METAL POLLUTION

We now know that children living in heavily lead-polluted areas (by busy motorways for instance, where the air is thick with exhaust fumes) develop learning and behavioural problems and that some hyperactive children who are treated for the removal of lead improve very quickly. Having a good standard of nutrition seems to be a protection against the effects of lead. Children deficient in magnesium, iron, Vitamin D, calcium or zinc are prone to being affected by lead. Nutritionists Drs. Stephen Davies and Alan Stewart, in their book Nutritional Medicine: The drug-free guide to better family health (published by Pan Books) quote an example:

"Anstey was an eight-year-old lad who was a bit of a tearaway at school. He came from a broken home and tended to be rather disruptive socially. One day, at breaktime, there was panic in the playground when Anstey tried to hang himself by his tie on the climbing frame. His father was called and he was taken home. The following day we arranged a mineral screen. It was found that his lead levels were twice the upper acceptable level, and his zinc level was one third the lower limit of normal. It was also evident that he was eating a lot of refined carbohydrates and junk food, and drinking a lot of colas. Here you have a situation of multiple nutrient deficiencies on the one hand, a high level of toxic metal and lots of artificial food additives on the other, in association with a presumably stressful domestic situation culminating in self-destructive behaviour. I spoke at length to Anstey and his father, and Anstey was given a multivitamin and mineral supplement with extra zinc and vitamin C, to correct the deficiencies and promote the excretion of lead. "He had acquired the lead, presumably, when he had been living in the Middle East with his father. Anstey became a much more manageable chap, seemed to enjoy life more, and subsequently did better at school."

Aluminium, too, is neuro-toxic, and behaviourally disturbed children are shown to have higher than normal levels of aluminium.

Drs. Davies and Stewart have this advice:
"We recommend that our patients avoid the use of aluminium cookware, and use, instead, Pyrex or glassware saucepans. Failing that you can use high-quality, enamel cookware, or even stainless steel. However, stainless steel saucepans are a rich source of nickel, and if you are nickel sensitive you should avoid using them.

"If it is impossible to replace your aluminium cookware with other pans, then try to keep at least one non-aluminium saucepan in which to cook vegetables or fruit. The acidic nature of these foods increases the degree to which aluminium can be scoured from inside the pan and incorporated in a soluble form into the food. By using an alternative pan for fruit and vegetables you will reduce the amount of aluminium you eat."

Never fill the kettle with water from the hot tap. It could contain high level of copper and possibly lead. It has been calculated that in London our drinking water has been recycled as much as nine times. It will of course be completely safe, hygienically, but has been liberally laced with chemicals in the process. Most of us suffer no ill effects. The hyperactive child, however, is more sensitive and therefore more susceptible than most.

Toxic levels of cadmium, aluminium and copper can be as damaging as lead; as are deficiencies of the minerals we require, such as calcium, iron, zinc and magnesium. It is as if not having enough of the correct elements leaves a space for the baddies to creep in.

Chemicals such as aerosol sprays, hanging fly killers,

paints, chlorine in swimming pool water are likely allergens. A water filter is often a reasonable way of coping with any heavy metals, organic pollutants and bacteria existing in the domestic supply.

IS THERE HYPERACTIVITY IN ADULTS?

The more experts you talk to on the subject of hyperactivity, the more complex the issue appears. "Children outgrow hyperactivity" is an often repeated diagnosis, suggesting that miraculously, come puberty, a child whose behaviour has been downright anti-social, who has lurched from crisis to crisis, who has known only ill health, who believes himself to be stupid and disruptive, because hasn't he been told so often enough, will suddenly, like someone awakening from a bad dream, become happy, healthy, co-operative and swiftly make up for all his previous learning problems in one mighty leap. Experience proves, sadly, that this is rarely the case. For the hyperactive, puberty brings a new set of problems to add to those he's carried all along.

Recently one of Sally Bunday's counsellors was approached by a young man of 25, who recognised in his own character and childhood experiences the hyperactive symptoms, was still experiencing periods of intense aggression and violence. He responded to advice and has solved his problem.

Since there is no wide scale research from which to draw conclusions, the scale of the problem is guesswork. On this basis, the HACSG believes as many as 25% of our children could suffer from hyperactivity or periodic symptoms created by food intolerance.

But it isn't only the hyperactivity that is the concern: these children are all below par in so many ways – endless throat infections, bad ears, constant tummy upsets. And why should so many be allergic, since this reflects the failure of the body's system to do its job properly, is a question that crops up over and over again.

Dr. Walter Barker of the Childhood Development Unit has this to say:

"We know that many allergies spring from early feeding. If the mother looks after her own health she can feed her baby herself with no need for anything else for the first four months. Then she should introduce other foods in very small quantities. Not a whole egg, but one drop of egg. Some vegetables from the family diet, pureed, just a teaspoon to make sure. Babies given too much of a food before they can adjust to it are high risk allergy sufferers.

"We should get away from this idea that baby food is something that comes out of a tin or jar labelled 'baby food'. Nature provides. Natural food – just what the family eats introduced slowly and increased a little every day as *part* of the baby's diet (beginning with fruit and vegetables of course, not steak and port chops!) along with breast milk gives the right start and saves so much bad health later."

Older children present a greater challenge, the baby can be supervised down to the last teaspoonful. The toddler is comparatively easy once you allow for 'accidents' of diet at friends' houses. Later the parent has to hope for co-operation since no eating regime can be imposed on a child at school and later, in their teens, it is even more difficult. The child whose problem has been identified at an early stage gets into a habit of healthy eating, gets to know his own body feelings and avoiding what upsets him becomes second nature. We (nearly) all, after all, learn to say no to the things that make us ill, whether it's too much red wine or surfeit of chocolates.

It isn't all gloom and doom.

When I first wrote about hyperactivity three years ago, one or two major food retailers were prepared to take a positive stand on the subject of additives. It seemed like a good idea to list in this book brands and retailing chains who were in tune with the problem. In the interim so many shops have taken positive steps towards reducing, eliminating, listing, guiding that the reasonably clued up shopper will have little difficulty in finding what she wants, additive free. Sainsbury, Safeway, Tesco, Waitrose, are all mindful of what they call "public concern" regarding food and all now have policies aimed at investigating and reducing suspect additives. However the customer still needs to be vigilant.

Beware, too, labels which say sugar-free when in fact they have substituted instead of sugar some chemical just as bad, if not worse. When in doubt, leave out seems a good maxim in this context. You don't actually NEED that suspect bottle of squash. The money could be far better spent.

And although there is little large-scale research into hyperactivity in children there is interest in research into the effects of food on behaviour of adults.

The level of aggression among inmates of an American prison fell dramatically when they were fed a healthy junk-free diet, and research coming in from numerous sources shows that where diets have been changed behaviour has changed too. We are talking about people in institutions such as detention centres for delinquents where it is practical to control diet and monitor the response. We are not talking about turning people into zombies, but turning them from aggressive, disorderly groups into normally behaved individuals. Now a corrective centre for delinquents in County Durham has instituted a programme of wholefood eating and will publish its findings in due course. As the Government has given its approval this is a hopeful sign of official co-operation and interest. For many of the "guinea pigs" it will be an experience, the chance to find out for themselves what it means to eat wholefood for the first time.

Sadly the traditional method of dealing with problem people in society is to lock them up, and even to dose them with drugs. Formerly little interest has been shown in prevention, even though preventative measures would cost a fraction of the total spent on dealing with the consequences of the problem.

The same is true of disorganised behaviour in children. If we were really interested in preventing the problems, in giving maximum support to the family of the seriously disorganised child, there would be three times as many workers in the child guidance field but huge savings in doctors – of inestimable value in real social terms.

This book has dealt mainly with hyperactivity and what parents can do about it. There is still a great deal not known and understood about the illness. For the moment mothers like Sally Bunday and her disciples who are fast setting up self-help groups throughout the country (there is the possibility of an HACSG clinic in the pipeline, funds permitting) and professionals like child psychologists are noting similarities.

It is a complicated and a complex problem. Medical explanations can be beyond the grasp of many of us.

One specialist, whom I asked how on earth he explained all this scientific stuff to his mothers, replied: "I rely on their common sense. If I tell them cut out the orange drink and he'll stop bed wetting and be a much happier boy tomorrow . . . they don't need me to tell them whether it's true or not. They can see for themselves."

You don't need blind faith, you can prove it for yourself. (At the risk of introducing a flippant note, but dog lovers will understand, I tackled my dog's hyperactive and thoroughly irritating restlessness which no amount of strenuous exercise could help, by taking him off tinned dog food, its rich brown colour unidentified on the label, and within forty eight hours he'd stopped rushing round in circles, yapping and nipping ankles and became thoroughly adorable).

Happy endings are always welcome. The dreadful Keiron who caused such despair to his elderly granny responded to the new diet, and with a few minor lapses thrived. He is the apple of her eye, a strong healthy 17-year-old, all the bad times behind him and a career in the Navy lined up.

The last word must go to Lynne who wrote from Norfolk.

"I wrote to you several weeks ago in desperation re my son Robert (nearly 10 yrs) I feel I must just write to you and tell you of the total transformation. "The first few days were sheer hell – not really as the food we were all eating was so different (I bake all my own bread, cakes, etc.) but orange squash, sweets, chocolate, were out. He was very 'anti' at first but we discussed it with him at length and he said he'd give it a go. Since those four first days on the diet he has been a different kid – he now says he used to feel "hot and angry" *all* the time – big spin off has been after spending years trundling from enuretic clinic to bell and buzzer to hypnotist – *dry nights* – he's so pleased – feels happy about going on the school summer trip. He's had the occasional wet bed – always following a dieting indiscretion which we've allowed occasionally – mainly to let him feel the difference. Easter was hell with choc. eggs from grandparents who "understood the diet" but "felt sorry for him" and as they were handed out at Easter and even more – cousins etc. were eating theirs – Robert had his – felt terrible the next day. Through trial and error have discovered all fruit and veg. are OK. Mint flavour is definitely out as of course artificial colours and flavouring, the preservative seems to be OK. His teacher actually came out of the school to see me at the end of term – "Well I don't know what to say about Robert." Oh God I thought, what's he done now (my usual age-old reaction) "He's a different child – actually *sits down* and *writes* – gets on OK with the other children – not constantly touching and irritating them." I can't tell you what this all means to me Sally. I can't count the number of times I've left school in tears after tales from other kids "Guess what the naughty boy did today" came wafting into earshot. "I can honestly say that for the first time over the last few weeks I can actually say I *like* Robert. He's calmer – no incredible mood swings – and a really super kid – if *only* I'd known about this years ago.

"I just wanted to write and let you know how we're getting on and to thank you – from all of us – for the difference it's making to all of us – I feel as if I can at last *enjoy* Robert – we're making up for 'lost' years at the rate of knots – and loving it."

THE GOOD FOODS AND THE BAD

The late Dr. Ben Feingold drew up a Food Programme.
In this, two separate groups were identified from the hyperactive child's diet, for four to six weeks.

Group A: All food and drink containing the suspect additives (as identified on pages 72–74).

Group B: Fruits and vegetables (fresh, frozen, dried or in tins) containing salicylate: These are almonds, apples, apricots, peas, peaches, plums, prunes, oranges, tomatoes, tangerines, cucumber, blackberries, strawberries, raspberries, gooseberries, cherries, currants, grapes and raisins.

If response is good, these fruits and vegetables may be introduced one at a time and, if there is still a good response, may be incorporated into the daily diet. Eliminating the fruits and vegetables may create a slight Vitamin C deficiency, so use instead 50 mg. Vitamin C tablets.

Red for Danger. Foods not allowed.

MEATS
　　Processed luncheon meats
　　Smoked meats
　　Bologna, salami
　　Frankfurters, sausages
　　Ham and bacon
　　Barbecued Meat and Poultry
　　Meat Pies (shop bought)

FISH
　　Smoked fish (i.e. smoked haddock/mackerel)
　　Kippers
　　Frozen fish with coloured coatings, i.e. fish fingers

DAIRY FOODS
   Flavoured/coloured Milkshakes
   Flavoured/coloured Yoghurt
   Coloured cheese
   Margarine with artificial colour
   Butter with artificial colour

BREADS/FLOURS
   White bread and flour have chemical additives and are best avoided
   Shop bought bakery good e.g. cakes, biscuits, pre-cooked pies, etc.
   Cereals with colour and flavours
   Packet mixes ... soup, sauces, cakes, puddings, etc.
   Porridge which may contain additives

VEGETABLES AND FRUITS
   Those given in Group 2, for 4-6 weeks (containing salicylates)
   Tinned vegetables and tinned fruit with colour

PRESERVES, JAMS, ETC.
   Shop bought jam and marmalade**
   Jellies, puddings, etc.
   Sweets, chocolates**
   Vanilla, Caramel and Mint flavours.
   Cider and wine vinegars
   Soy sauce, chilli sauce
   Sweet/savoury bought sauces
   Gravy mixes, stock cubes**

MEDICINES
   Aspirin
   Cough sweets and pastilles
   Coloured sweets and tablets
   Alka Selzer
   Flavoured toothpaste

MISCELLANEOUS
- Flavoured crisps
- Tea. Coffee. Instant mix drinks
- Soft drinks/squashes (with colours, etc.)
- Cider, beer, wine
- 'Diet' drinks.

Green for Go. Foods allowed

MEATS
- Fresh meats (all)
- Offal
- Poultry, fresh or frozen
- Frozen carcase meats.

Some minced fresh meat contains preservative, so ask before you buy.

FISH
- Fresh fish
- Fresh shell fish
- Frozen white fish
- Tinned fish in oil or brine

DAIRY FOODS
- Fresh milk
- Plain/natural yoghurt
- Some margarines**
- Some butters**
- White cheeses, without flavourings.

BREADS/FLOURS
- Wholemeal bread and flour (81%-100% stoneground if possible)
- Wholemeal pasta
- Homemade bakery goods, e.g. cakes
- Biscuits
- Porridge**

Some shop bought biscuits**
ANY cereals without colour flavours

VEGETABLES
ALL fresh/frozen vegetables
(Except those in Group 2 for 4-6 weeks)
Some tinned in water only
Some dried vegetables.

FRUITS
(Except those in Group 2 for 4-6 weeks)
Fresh and Frozen
Banana, Pear, Lemon, Grapefruit, Melon, Pineapple, Guave, Avocado, Rhubarb
Figs (fresh/dried)
Some fruits tinned in own syrup

PRESERVES, JAMS, ETC.
Homemade jam, marmalade
Pure honey
Homemade sweets/ice creams/lollies made with permitted fruit juices and plain gelatin
White vinegar
Homemade pickles
Some shop sweets** on 'Safe' list

MISCELLANEOUS
Plain unflavoured crisps**
Some nuts**
Homemade drinks etc. made from permitted fruit jucices
Barley Cup   7 UP

**THE 'SAFE' FOOD LIST GIVES ALTERNATIVES.

HACSG 'Safe' food list.

Below is a typical list which Sally Bunday mails on a regular basis to members. However, foods change, some become safer, others, paradoxically, suddenly acquire an unacceptable additive.

Red for Danger

More than one hundred years ago an eminent chemist wrote a book on the Treatise on Adulteration of Food and Culinary Poisons, sub-headed There is Death in the Pot. It became an instant best seller and drew attention to such practices as adding chalk to the flour and chemical dyes to the wine. Manufacturers insisted that additives enhanced the taste and appearance of their food and this was what the public wanted. The public said otherwise and there was a long (over thirty years) battle to get the government to pass the Sale of Food and Drugs Act, which stated that it was an offence to sell food "not of the nature, substance or quality of the article demanded". Our present legislation is based on that Act. The 1984 Act took it further and legislated procedures for food labelling.

Many people believe that the additives we have in our daily diet are unnecessary and potentially harmful. For the moment they are a fact of life so it is worth identifying them and learning to spot them on the labels (given good eyesight, and never go shopping without your specs). Many (not *all*) additives cause discomfort generally such as migraine, itchy rashes, gastric irritation, nausea, vertigo. In this instance we are concerned with children and causes of or contributory factors to hyperactivity.

Additives which may contribute to HYPERACTIVITY

E102 E104 107 E110 E120 E122 E124 E127
128 E131 E132 133 E150 E151 154 155 E210
E211 E212 E213 E214 E215 E216 E217 E218 E219
E220 E250 E251 E310 E311 E312 E320 E321 621
622 627 631 635

Additives which may contribute to ALLERGY-TYPE symptoms, e.g. skin rashes, itching, wheezing, runny nose.

E102 107 E110 E122 E123 E124 E127 E131 E132
 155 E210 E211 E212 E213 E214 E215 E216 E217
E218 E219 E221 E222 E223 E310 E311 E312

You will notice that all the numbers in the second group, except for 221-3 appear also in the first group.

The forty four different numbers in these two groups may seem daunting to avoid, but we are helped by the fact that only eighteen of them are encountered with any frequency and of those only about a dozen very frequently.

The potentially harmful additives that we commonly come across (in such foods as) are:

E102 (tinned processed peas, packet dessert topping, fizzy drinks),
E110 (Hot chocolate mix, packet soup, Swiss roll, Lemon curd)
E122 (Packet soup mix, packet jellies)
E123 (Liquid vitamin C preparations, Gravy granules, Tinned fruit pie fillings)
E124 (Packet trifle mix, packet cake mix, dessert topping, quick setting jelly mix)
 128 (Frankfurters)
E132 (Savoury convenience food mix)
 133 (Tinned processed peas)
E150 (Chocolate dessert whip, savoury convenience food mix, prepacked cakes, soya sauce.)
E210 (Jams, beer, flavouring syrups, marinated herring and mackerel, salad cream and dressing.)
E211 (Margarine, barbecue sauce, cheesecake mix, orange squash)
E220 (Packet soup, blackcurrant jam, fruit-based milk and cream desserts, fruit-based pie fillings, dehydrated vegetables)

E223 (Orange squash, packet mashed potatoes)
E250 (Salted meat to fix the red colour, tinned meat, frozen pizza)
E320 (Biscuits, sweets, savoury rice, packet convenience foods)
E321 (Packet cake mix, crisps, salted peanuts, dry breakfast cereals)
621 (Packet snacks, pork pies, packet soup and quick soups)

Those in bold are the most common.

A number of these additives are chemically related to the compound which constitutes aspirin, so when embarking on a diet to exclude these additives it is also important to refrain from giving your child anything which may contain aspirin (e.g. Junior Disprin).

So where does that take us? When the London Food Commission produced its guidelines for supervisors and catering staff in charge of under-fives, it came up with some common sense rules for healthier happy children. Plan to make changes over a period of weeks rather than days.

Red for Danger:

Snacks	Salty food, crisps nuts. Sweet food, cakes, biscuits sweets. Sweet drinks, squashes.
Meals	Sausages, bacon, meat pies and pastries. Fruit canned in heavy syrup. Suet puddings, sweet custards, cream, synthetic whips
Cooking methods	Peeling edible fruit and veg skins Long boiling Frying and deep frying Roasting.

Green for Go:

Snacks
: Wholegrain bread, rolls, pita, peanut butter (smooth)
Fruit and dried fruit
Popcorn (plain)
Pure fruit juices (diluted)

Meals
: Freshly-made soup, pasta
Potatoes and starchy veg. (not fried or roast)
Beans, lentils, dahl, rice
All sorts of veg. raw or lightly cooked
Fish (fresh or frozen) chicken, lean meat
Fruit pies (pastry, crumble, etc. made with wholemeal flour and unsaturated fat)
Low-fat yoghurt, with own-added fruit.

Cooking Methods
: Washing and cutting veg. just before needed
Light boiling, poaching, steaming and stir-frying.
Baking.

"Maybe it is time we destroyed the myth that left to their own devices children choose 'junk' food" wrote one Under Fives Nursery chef, reporting little difficulty in getting children to accept the new diet. Two weeks of sample menus from that particular day nursery follow.

Menu 1	Breakfast	Lunch	Tea
Monday	Cereals: Shredded wheat, Muesli, All Bran Weetabix. Wholemeal toast Fresh orange Juice.	Quiche Lorraine Boiled potatoes Green beans Bakewell tart Custard	Homemade fish cakes Lemon souffle
Tuesday	as above	Beef curry with rice Chocolate sponge white sauce.	Pilchards on toast Fresh fruit.
Wednesday	as above	Welsh eggs Salad and jacket potatoes Lemon yogurt.	Soup and baps Carrot cake
Thursday	as above	Pastie, cabbage, carrots and turnip, gravy Rice pudding and stewed apples	Tuna sandwiches Peanut butter and crackers
Friday	as above	Lentil and barley broth and rolls Apple crumble and custard.	Pizza Bran loaf

Many of the meals include usual nursery dishes, but the ingredients are always fresh and not refined.

Menu 2	Breakfast	Lunch	Tea
Monday	Cereals: Shredded wheat, Muesli, All Bran, Weetabix. Wholemeal toast Fresh orange juice.	Egg and onion lasagne Luscious lemon cake.	Vegetable pate toast Wholemeal biscuits.
Tuesday	as above	Cod, white sauce Boiled potatoes. Carrots Chocolate eclairs	Cheese and tomato pizza Brown sugar meringues
Wednesday	as above	Homity pies Sprouts and carrots Fresh fruit salad	Green pea soup, wholemeal baps. Melting moments.
Thursday	as above	Winter hot pot Apple pie and white sauce	Egg mayonnaise sandwiches with salad Bran loaf.
Friday	as above	Vegetable hot pot cobbler Uncooked lemon cheesecake	Tomato toasts Assorted fresh fruits

THE SWEET BAG

Grateful mothers have, over the years, written to the HACSG with their own tried and trusted recipes. You will note a preponderance of those yummy sweet things we find it so hard to give up, and many are easy enough for the children (with a little adult supervision) to make themselves.

Honey Banana Lollies

½ Banana
1 tablespoon honey
1 tablespoon chopped nuts.
Place a lolly stick or teaspoon handle in the banana. Spread honey over banana. Roll in nuts and freeze.

Lemon Curd

¼ lb. Vitaseig (whey-free margarine)
½ lb. fruit sugar
3 lemons
4 yolks or 2 whole eggs.
Grate lemon rind and strain lemon juice. Put all ingredients into a saucepan and stir over a very gentle heat until thick and smooth. Pour into dry warm jars. Tie down and store in a cool, dry place.

Soya Cream Using a Bel Cream Maker

4 oz. Vitaseig
4 oz. soya milk (sugar free).
Make to instructions with cream maker. If for one, use 1 oz. of each, or two if you want to keep a bit for next day.

Soya Ice Cream with Apple

Make ½ pint Soya Cream.
1 lb. cooking apples, stewed with fruit sugar
2 teasp. lemon juice
1 oz. Vitaseig
2 eggs, separated
2 oz. fruit sugar.
Sieve or puree stewed fruit and add whisked egg yolks. Whisk egg whites until stiff, adding sugar. Fold egg whites and cream (cream first) into the puree and freeze. Thaw for ½-¾ hour before serving and whip in a mixer.

Banana Milk Shake

1 small banana, sliced
⅓ pt. soya milk
1 dessertspoon maple syrup.
Put all ingredients into a processor. Process on 3 till blended.

Lemon Surprise

1 lemon
2 oz. fruit sugar
2 oz. Vitaseig
2 eggs, separated
½ pt. sugar free soya milk
2 oz. wholemeal flour.

Whisk egg whites until stiff. Beat margarine, egg yolk, sugar and lemon peel. Stir in milk, lemon juice and fold in flour. Fold this batter into the egg whites. Put in ovenproof dish. Stand in a dish containing a little water. Bake at 200 dg. C for 40-45 mins. or until light brown and firm.

Rich Banana Bread

4 oz. Vitaseig
5 oz. fruit sugar
1 egg
5 oz. wholemeal flour
2½ oz. rice flour
½ tsp. bicarb
½ tsp. cream of tartar
½ tsp. salt
2 large bananas
3 tsp. soya cream.

Mash bananas and cream (using processor), process all ingredients on speed 3. Bake at 180 deg. C.

Shortcrust pastry

5 oz. White Flora
2 tbs. cold water
8 oz. wholemeal flour.
Cream Flora and water together. Cut flour in with a round ended knife. Put in the fridge for ½ an hour. Knead till smooth. Roll out as required.

Lemon Granes

4 oz. fruit sugar
1 pt. water
thinly pared rind and the juice of 3 lemons
4 lemon twists to decorate.
Gently heat the sugar and water in a pan until sugar dissolves. Then boil for 5 mins. Add lemon juice. Cool and strain. Pour into a rigid freezer container. Cover and seal and freeze for 2 hours. Whisk and return to the freezer for a further 2 hours. Whisk again and return to the freezer till firm. Leave at room temperature for 10 minutes, then stir until crumbly.

Yorkshire Pudding

2 heaped dessertspoons wholemeal flour
salt, pepper to taste
1 egg; ½ pt. water.
Beat egg and water into dry ingredients.

Rhubarb Puffs

Stewed rhubarb (or apple, peeled) into 6 small ovenproof dishes
3 eggs, separated
2 tsp fruit sugar
1½ tsp wholemeal flour.
Beat egg yolks and flour till smooth. Whisk egg white until stiff. Add sugar. Fold in egg yolk mixture. Spoon over fruit and bake at 350 deg. F 180 deg. C, Gas 2, for 10-15 minutes till risen.

Victoria Sponge.

4 oz. wholemeal flour
½ tsp. bicarb
½ tsp. cream of tartar
2 oz. fruit sugar
2 eggs, separated
a little soya milk (sugar free)
4 oz. Vitaseig.
Beat egg yolk into a creamed margarine, sugar. Add a little milk. Fold in flour, then fold in beaten egg whites. Makes small cakes or a large sponge. Soak finished sponge in maple syrup overnight for a different flavour. Bake at 180 deg. C. for 35-40 mins. To make butterfly cakes, mix 2 tsp. White Flora with 2 tsp. maple syrup (needs to be an electric mixer).

Breakfast Cereal

4 oz. toasted oats
1 oz. toasted wheat germ
2 oz. chopped hazel nuts
4 oz. chopped dates
2 oz. desiccated coconut
1 oz. banana crisps
1 oz. toasted sunflower seeds.
Mix and serve with soya milk and fruit sugar or honey.

Crunchy topping for ice cream, fruit or salad.

3 oz. oats
1 oz. fruit sugar
2 oz. Vitaseig
2 oz. wheat germ or nuts (hazel, peanuts or cashew)
1 oz. sunflower seeds.
Melt margarine in a heavy pan. Add ingredients and stir continuously till brown. Keep in a sealed container in the fridge for weeks.

Salad

1 stick of celery
1 onion
small piece each of red and green pepper.
Chop finely and mix.

Wholewheat Crumble

Stewed fruit
3 oz. fruit sugar
6 oz. wholemeal flour
1 tsp. bicarbonate of soda
1 tsp cream of tartar
3 oz. Vitaseig pinch of salt.
Combine dry ingredients. Rub in margarine. Spread over fruit and bake at 170 deg. C for 30 mins.

Lemonade

2 pts. boiling water
3 oz. fruit sugar
2 lemons.
Peel lemon finely. Only the thin rind. Add rind to boiling water with sugar and the juice. Leave to cool. Strain. Keep refrigerated. Makes good lollies.

Lemon Barley

2 pts. water
2 lemons
3 oz. barley
3 oz. fruit sugar.
Rinse barley. Add to water. Simmer for 10 minutes and strain off barley. Add finely peeled rind of lemons, sugar and juice of lemons to strained barley water. Cool and strain. Refrigerate.

Vegetable Soup

Chicken stock cube
1 carrot
2 leeks
stick celery
1 potato.
Chop all vegetables. Add to stock. Bring to boil. Simmer and add salt and pepper.

USEFUL ADDRESSES

Hyperactive Children's Support Group, (HCSG),
Sally Bunday, 71 Whyke Lane, Chichester, Sussex.
PO19 2LD (Letters only)
Telephone: 0903 725182

(Always send a s.a.e. when writing).

Companies making additive free vitamin supplements etc.

Associated Preparations, Larkhall Laboratories
225 Putney Bridge Road, London SW15 2PY

Makers of Junamac, (complete vitamin and mineral supplement for children up to 12 years) and other supplements.

Bio Health Ltd.
13 Oakdale Road, London SW16 2HP
(Will send sample of some of their vitamins etc. to 'allergy' sufferers for testing)

Nature's Own
51 Rodney Road,
Cheltenham, Gloucestershire.

Nature's Best.
Freepost P.O. Box 1 Tunbridge Wells,
TE1 1XQ

Shaklee International.
Central Milton Keynes MK9 2LS

Shaklee Products cover additive free nutritional supplements, personal care products and biodegradeable household cleaners, etc. They are bought through independent distributors.

FURTHER READING

E for Additives
   by Maurice Hanssen
   Published by Thorsons. £2.95

Additives – Your Complete Survival Guide.
   by Felicity Lawrence
   Published by Century Hutchinson. £3.95

The Zinc Solution.
   by Professor Derek Bruce-Smith and Liz Hodgkinson
   Published by Century Arrow. £3.50

Nutritional Medicine, The Drug Free guide to Better Family Health.
   by Dr Stephen Davies and Dr. Alan Stewart.
   Published by Pan Books. £3.95

Happiness is Junk-Free Food
   by Janet Ash and Dulcie Roberts
   Published by Thorsons

NOTES

NOTES

NOTES

NOTES

NOTES

NOTES

NOTES

NOTES